WELLINGTON SQUARE

PC Kent and 'The Detectives'

John and Marilyn Talbot

Illustrated by Mike Lacey

Reinforcement Readers

Rocky was looking out of the school window. He was surprised to see a police car come into the school.

'The police are here,' he said to Jamila.
'Has someone been bad?'

Mr Belter smiled.
'No-one has been bad,' he said. 'PC Kent is going to talk to you all.'

The Head Teacher came in with PC Kent.
'We are very pleased to have PC Kent in school with us,' she said.
'He is going to tell us what it is like to be a policeman.'

‘This is good,’ said Jamila.
‘I like PC Kent,’ said Ben.

PC Kent began to talk to the children.
He began to tell them lots of things.
He told them about his police car.
He told them about his police dog.

He had a torch and a police radio.
He let Jamila try them out.
Jamila smiled. She was very pleased.

PC Kent told them how he had to find missing children and take them home.

He told them how he had to catch bad people!

‘PC Kent is brave,’ said Rocky.
‘He is my favourite policeman,’ said Kevin.

Then PC Kent smiled.
'I am pleased to be a policeman,' he said. 'I think I am a good policeman, but now I will tell you something that made me look very silly.'
The children were surprised.
They all listened.

PC Kent went on.
'One day I was in Wellington Square, when I saw a man stealing a bag from a little old lady. She screamed and the man ran off.'

““I must catch him,” I thought, and I quickly ran after him.

‘I grabbed the man and pushed him down.
He was surprised.
But then I was surprised!

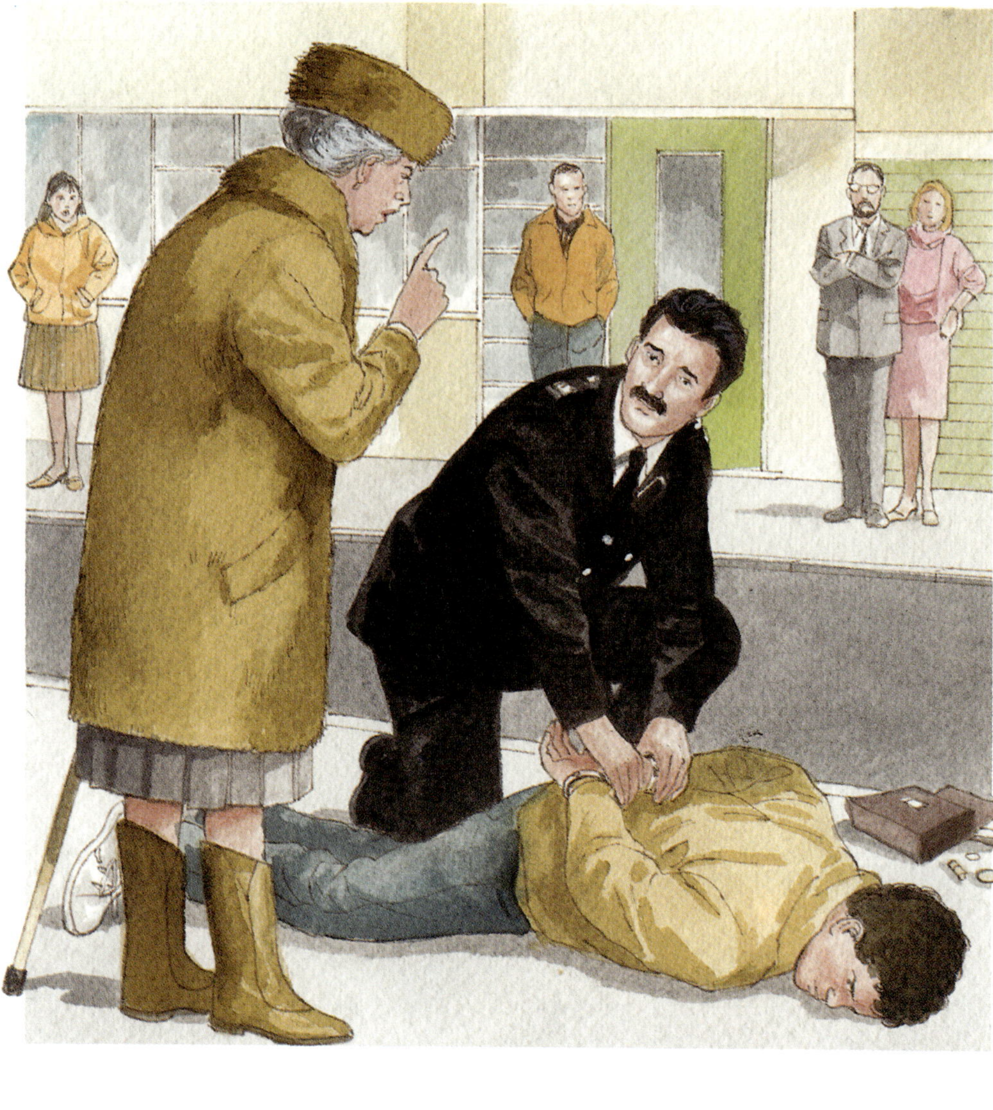

‘The little old lady wasn’t pleased at all.
Lots of other people were watching me and they were not pleased.

‘A man ran up to me.
“What do you think you are doing?” he shouted.
“This man was stealing her bag,” I said.

““Yes, he did try to steal her bag,” the man shouted. “He is in a television show. It’s called ‘The Detectives’. Look!”

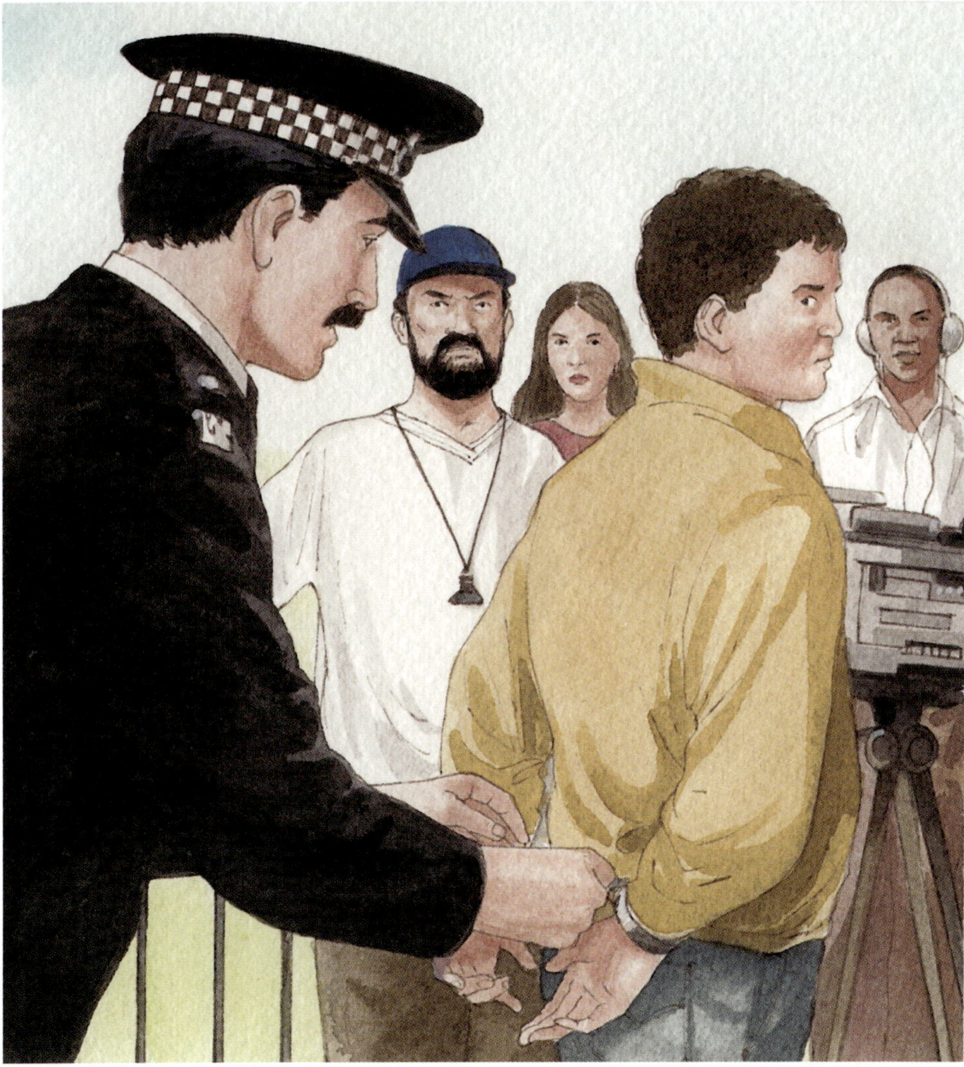

‘Then I saw that they were making a television show in Wellington Square.
“I’m afraid I didn’t know,” I said. “No-one told me”.’

‘You did look silly,’ said Kevin.
‘I know,’ said PC Kent.

Then all the other children wanted to
say something.
They all asked PC Kent something.

'What is your favourite food?' asked Ben.
'Chicken and chips,' said PC Kent.

'What is your favourite sport?' asked Kevin.
'Football,' said PC Kent.
'And what is your favourite television show?'
asked Tessa.

‘ “The Detectives”! ’ said PC Kent, and smiled!